LEVEL 2

D0091812

Coral Reefs

Kristin Baird Rattini

NATIONAL GEOGRAPHIC

Washington, D.C.

To Katie and Ryan —K. B. R.

Editor: Shelby Alinsky
Art Director: Amanda Larsen
Editorial: Snapdragon Books
Designer: YAY! Design
Photo Editor: Lori Epstein
Production Assistants: Sanjida Rashid and Rachel Kenny
Rights Clearance Specialist: Michael Cassady
Manufacturing Manager: Rachel Faulise

The author and publisher gratefully acknowledge the expert content review of this book by Roger Beeden, manager of ecosystem resilience, Great Barrier Reef Marine Park Authority, and the literacy review of this book by Mariam Jean Dreher, professor of reading education, University of Maryland, College Park.

Photo Credits
Abbreviations: CO = Corbis; GI = Getty Images; NGC = National Geographic Creative; SS = Shutterstock
Cover, Jane Gould/Alamy; 1, Paul Sutherland/NGC; 3, Piero Malaer/iStockphoto; 4-5, David Doubilet/NGC; 6, 145/Georgette Douwma/Ocean/CO; 7, NG Maps; 8, Norbert Wu/Minden Pictures; 8 (INSET), Jon Bertsch/Visuals Unlimited/CO; 9 (UP), Birgitte Wilms/Minden Pictures; 9 (LO), Birgitte Wilms/Minden Pictures; 10 (INSET), Jurgen Freund/Nature Picture Library; 10, Clay Bryce/SeaPics.com; 12, Vilainecrevette/Alamy; 12-13, Reinhard Dirscherl/SeaPics.com; 13, L. Newman & A. Flowers/Science Source; 14, Paul Sutherland/NGC; 15 (UPLE), Jim Abernethy/NGC; 15 (UPRT), Paul Sutherland/NGC; 15, Alex Mustard/Nature Picture Library; 16 (LE), Visuals Unlimited, Inc./Reinhard Dirscherl/GI; 16 (RT), David Fleetham/Alamy; 17, Reinhard Dirscherl/Alamy; 18 (UP), Ethan Daniels/SeaPics.com; 18 (LO), blickwinkel/Alamy; 19, David Peart/arabian-Eye/GI; 20 (UP), Beverly Speed/SS; 20 (LO), Chris Newbert/Minden Pictures; 21 (UP), Joseph Dovala/WaterFrame RM/GI; 21 (INSET), Norbert Wu/Minden Pictures; 22 (UP), Ethan Daniels/SS; 22 (CTR), Pete Oxford/Minden Pictures; 22 (LO), Franco Banfi/WaterFrame RM/GI; 23 (UP), WaterFrame/Image-broker RF/GI; 23 (CTR), courtesy Owen Sherwood/University of Colorado; 23 (LO), Oliver Lucanus/NiS/Minden Pictures; 24-25, Mark A. Johnson/CO; 26, Brian J. Skerry/NGC; 27, Maritime Safety Queensland/GI; 29, Stephen Frink/CO; 30 (UP), David Doubilet/NGC; 30 (CTR), amana images inc./Alamy; 30 (LO A), BlueOrange Studio/SS; 30 (LO B), Andrea Izzotti/SS; 30 (LO C), eastern light photography/SS; 30 (LO D), Stephen Frink/Digital Vision; 31 (UP), Franco Banfi/Nature Picture Library; 31 (CTR RT), Ball Miwako/Alamy; 31 (CTR LE), Stephen Frink/Digital Vision; 31 (LO), Michael Patrick O'Neill/Science Source; 32 (UPLE), blickwinkel/Alamy; 32 (UPRT), Visuals Unlimited, Inc./Reinhard Dirscherl/GI; 32 (CTR LE), Jon Bertsch/Visuals Unlimited/CO; 32 (CTR RT), 145/Georgette Douwma/Ocean/CO; 32 (LOLE), NG Maps; 32 (LORT), Maritime Safety Queensland/GI; top border (throughout), Transia Design/SS; vocabulary box art, Incomible/SS

**National Geographic supports K–12 educators with ELA Common Core Resources.
Visit natgeoed.org/commoncore for more information.**

Printed in the United States of America
19/WOR/6

Table of Contents

City Under the Sea

The shallow ocean waters look calm. But under the surface, a coral reef is a busy place.

Hundreds, even thousands, of different creatures swim and hide along the reef. There they find food and shelter. They make their home in this "city under the sea."

A coral reef is a very important ecosystem (EE-koh-sis-tum). More sea creatures live along coral reefs than in any other part of the ocean.

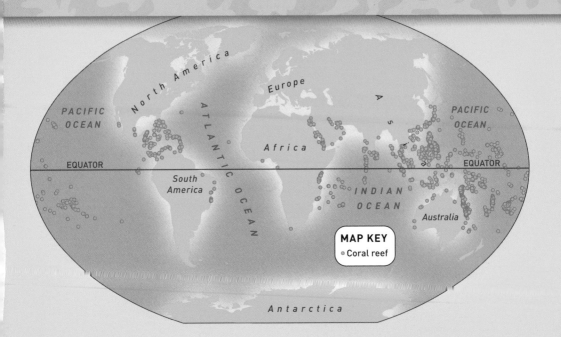

Reefs are found in many spots around the world. Most reefs grow in shallow, clean ocean waters on either side of the Equator (i-KWAY-tur). They need sunlight and warm temperatures year-round to survive.

Reef Builders

a group of
coral polyps

a coral polyp
up close

Coral reefs
look like they are
made of rocks. But, in fact, they are
groups of animals called corals.
Each coral group is made up of many
separate coral polyps (POL-ips).

In reef ecosystems, there are two kinds of coral: hard and soft. Only hard coral polyps form reefs. They're named for the hard skeletons they build at the base of their soft bodies.

Hard corals make reefs.

Soft corals do not make reefs.

Reef Talk

CORAL POLYP: a small, simple sea animal with a tube-shaped body and a mouth ringed with tentacles at the top

One coral polyp can be as small as the head of a pin. But when many polyps join together, they make a reef that can stretch for miles.

fan coral with open polyps

New polyps build their hard skeletons on top of old ones. Over many years, these layers of skeletons slowly grow into a coral reef.

hard coral reef

In the Zone

All coral reefs have three zones. The reef flat zone often stretches toward land. The crest zone is the highest part of the reef. The reef slope zone faces the open ocean. It's the deepest part of the reef.

reef flat zone

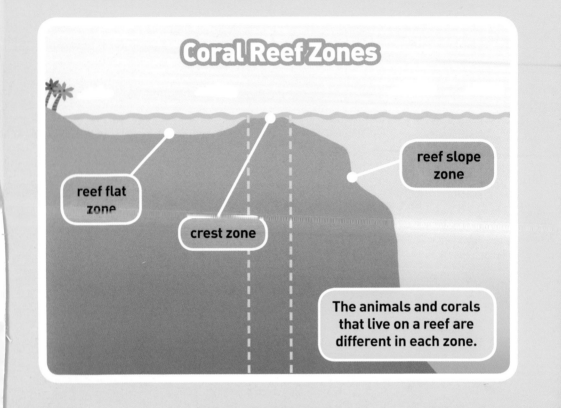

Coral Reef Zones

reef flat zone

crest zone

reef slope zone

The animals and corals that live on a reef are different in each zone.

crest zone

reef slope zone

Neighbors on the Reef

Creatures big and small can be found on reefs around the world. Sea stars travel slowly along a reef's surface. Giant clams rest there too. Tube sponges stretch up from a reef like small chimneys. Seahorses wrap their tails around pieces of coral. Sea turtles swim around reefs. Eels hide in a reef's cracks.

sea star

tube sponges

seahorse

giant clam

Many animals use camouflage
(KAM-uh-flazh) to hide along the
reef. Some use it to stay safe from
other animals that could eat them.
Others use it
to hide while
they hunt.

reef stonefish

trumpetfish

cuttlefish

A stonefish's bumpy body blends in with the coral. A trumpetfish dives down and holds still. Its long, thin body stretches up like a tall sponge. A cuttlefish can change its shape and skin color to match the coral reef.

Reef Plants

Plants play an important role in coral reef ecosystems.

Tiny algae (AL-jee) live inside the coral polyps' soft bodies. The algae use sunlight to make food for the coral. This helps the coral grow.

algae that grow inside coral polyps, as seen through a microscope

Sea grass can grow in the reef flat zone. It helps trap mud from rivers that flow into the ocean. Sea grass also provides food for dugongs and sea turtles.

Reef Talk

ALGAE: Simple plants without stems or leaves that grow in or near water

dugong

The Reef in Darkness

longspine squirrelfish

As night falls, life along the reef changes. Different animals come out to find food.

octopus

Caribbean reef sharks

cone snail

Squirrelfish use their large eyes to search for shrimp in the darkness. Octopuses stretch their arms over the reef to feel for food. Sharks hunt for fish. Cone snails catch fish and worms.

6 COOL FACTS
About Coral Reefs

1 There are more than 800 different kinds of hard coral in the world's oceans.

Brain corals can live for 900 years.

2

3 The first coral reefs on Earth formed 240 million years ago, before dinosaurs were alive.

Most coral reefs today are between 5,000 and 10,000 years old.

4

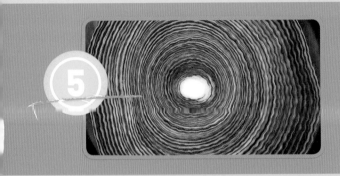

5

Corals have growth rings, just like trees.

The Great Barrier Reef is off Australia's northeast coast. It is the largest coral reef system on Earth. It can be seen from space!

6

People and Reefs

Coral reefs are important to more than just animals and plants. They are important to people, too.

Millions of people eat the fish that live along reefs.

Many people earn money from fishing or taking tourists to visit reefs.

Reefs also help protect people and houses on land. They block big waves from crashing on the shore.

Rescuing Reefs

dead coral

Many reefs are in danger. Scientists are worried about threats to coral reefs.

Ocean waters around the world are getting warmer. Coral polyps die when the water is too warm.

Pollution (puh-LOO-shun) sometimes spills into the oceans. It can harm reefs.

Fishing and boating can also damage fragile reefs.

The *Shen Neng 1* struck the Great Barrier Reef in 2010. The ship scraped along the reef for almost two miles, damaging coral and spilling oil into the water.

But there is good news.
Many people are working
to save reefs.

Volunteers help clean up
pollution on land and at sea.
Some countries have special
areas, called preserves, where
coral reefs are protected.

Divers and swimmers—
like you—can help, too!
The next time you see
a beautiful coral reef, look
but don't touch.

QUIZ WHIZ

How much do you know about coral reefs? After reading this book, probably a lot! Take this quiz and find out.

Answers are at the bottom of page 31.

1

What are coral reefs made of?

A. hard coral polyps
B. rocks
C. soft coral polyps
D. none of the above

2

Which zone is found on the highest part of the reef?

A. the reef flat zone
B. the crest zone
C. the reef slope zone
D. the end zone

Which of these animals does not live along a coral reef?

A. eel
B. horse
C. sea star
D. giant clam

3

4

Which of these animals can be found along reefs at night?

A. cone snail
B. octopus
C. shark
D. all of the above

Earth's largest coral reef system is off the coast of which country?

A. Australia
B. Belize
C. Indonesia
D. United States

5

6

How old are most coral reefs today?

A. 5,000 to 10,000 years old
B. 50,000 years old
C. 500,000 years old
D. 500 million years old

What can be harmful to coral reefs?

A. fishing and boating
B. pollution
C. rising water temperatures
D. all of the above

7

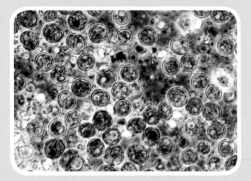

ALGAE: simple plants without stems or leaves that grow in or near water

CAMOUFLAGE: an animal's natural color or shape that helps it hide from other animals

CORAL POLYP: a small, simple sea animal with a tube-shaped body and a mouth ringed with tentacles at the top

ECOSYSTEM: all the living and nonliving things in an area

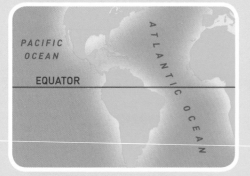

EQUATOR: the imaginary line around Earth halfway between the North and South Poles

POLLUTION: harmful matter that makes water, soil, or air dirty